THE BOY IN BUCHENWALD

A Victim's Survival Story

R.T. Watts

KNOWLEDGE BOOKS

Teacher Notes:

In this inspirational and true survival story, Steffan, a Polish teenage boy, finds himself imprisoned during World War 2 in Buchenwald, a Nazi concentration camp. Steffan's recount of the things he did to stay alive seems both incredible and unbelievable. This story also explains the terrible suffering endured by people simply because of their views, their faith, or their birthplace.

Discussion Points for Consideration:

1. Why were Jewish people sent to the Nazi concentration camps?

2. What does the word Holocaust mean?

3. What happened to the Nazis after the Holocaust?

Difficult words to be introduced and practiced before reading the book:

Barracks, Buchenwald, Nazi, concentration, Germany, factories, former, soldiers, starving, tongues, bombers, prisoners, explosion, forgiven, capture, experiment, Jewish, political, disinfected, separated, factories, survive, conditions, injection, Americans.

SENSITIVITY NOTICE:

This book is not suitable for a young reader. Restriction should be considered based on age. Adolescent readers will find the topic confronting and disturbing. Prior notice before reading should be considered.

Contents

This is not my story. This story was told to me by a man named Steffan 30 years ago. I was honored that he thought me worthy to talk with for a day. He wanted me to write his story. I am sorry to Steffan that it has taken so long.

This story is about Poland during World War II and what happened to Steffan in the concentration camps. It is not a happy story but tells how important it is to try hard to get what you need. Steffan lived through hell, but he never gave up.

3

1. Poland

Poland was my home. I was just 15 years old when the war started. In 1939, Poland was attacked by Germany on one side and by Russia on the other.

Poland had great land for growing food and plenty of factories. Both sides wanted to take these border areas for themselves.

Poland fought hard but two big armies on each side was too much. We were crushed!

The Germans took over the area
where I lived. All Jewish people were
made to wear a yellow star badge on
their front and back. They had to wear
the yellow star every time they left the
house.

I saw boys my own age wearing these
badges. Even very young children
had to wear the badge.

2. Hitler

Adolf Hitler was the leader of Germany. He had formed his own political group called the Nazi Party. He told the German people that they would be much better off under his rule.

Many Germans were still hungry and poor. These people were promised they would be much better off, with plenty of food. Hitler spent a lot of money and blamed Germany's problems on Jewish people and on other countries.

The people had been lied to. Hitler took them on the road to hell. Hitler's simple answers sounded good but running a country is very hard. There are so many things to do and plan. One person cannot do all this!

Everyone has problems and needs help at some time. Hitler was telling everyone he was the answer. He got a lot of money from banks and spent it mostly on building up the army and air force. This made the German people think he was very smart. The money was never repaid, and the country was still poor.

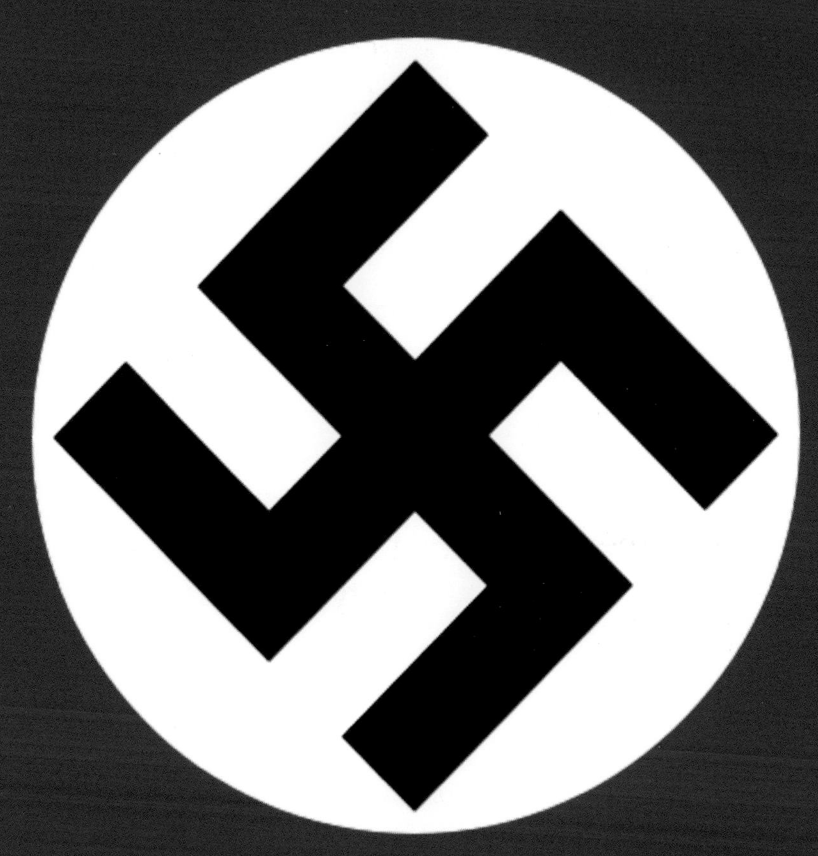

3. Farm Work

The Germans were now in control of my part of Poland. I was taken from my home and forced to go to Germany to work on a farm. I worked in the potato fields.

I had to pull out weeds from the potato fields. I also picked the potatoes from the soil. I worked every day on the farm.

4. Escape

I was young and did not understand why I was being worked all the time. The Germans were no longer just at war with Poland. Now they were at war with Britain, France, and their former friend, Russia.

I talked with a friend I had made at the farm, and we decided to escape. One night, when we were still working, we ran from the potato field. We got to a small town and looked to catch a train back to Poland.

We waited for the train, hoping no one would notice we had gone. As the train arrived, we saw the guards pointing towards us. Some soldiers came and grabbed us.

5. Capture and Train Journey

The soldier that caught me told me I was not going back to the farm. Instead, I was put on a train. I did not know where I was going.

I heard them trying to work out where I should be sent. I saw Jewish people at the train station. Men, women, and little children were all being forced onto trains. Where were these people going?

I did not know it at the time, but I was being sent to a prison. It was a prison for anyone that Hitler did not want. Any person or people who were seen as a problem were being sent to these prisons.

These prisons were called concentration camps. Jewish people, Roma people, political prisoners, Russian soldiers, children, and me! "Why me?" I asked.

I told the soldier I was just a Polish boy. All I did was go into the town. I cried to him, but he could do nothing.

6. Buchenwald

I arrived at the concentration camp and was put into a hut with a lot of beds. I was with a lot of men. There were no other boys my age.

I had a blanket and was given some bread and soup. We had nothing else. It was quiet. Everyone was being careful and thinking about food.

I was disinfected and sprayed to stop lice from spreading. The Germans were trying to stop disease killing everyone.

Berlin
Germany
Buchenwald

At the start, we were separated from the Jewish men. They were not part of our barracks. This changed as the people in the barracks changed.

We worked in the camp factories making gun parts. At night we were given our food and sent back to the barracks. Sometimes I found other food on the way back from the factories.

7. The Hunger

It is hard to imagine being hungry all the time. It feels like something is eating you from the inside. I could never stop thinking about food.

The food they gave us was not enough for us to survive. We would die in 3-6 months. It was meant to kill us slowly!

We worked and needed food to stay alive. The prison people knew exactly how long we would be able to work before dying.

When you are starving, your body first uses up all the fat on your arms and legs. It then uses all the fat between your organs. After this, your flesh and muscles start to go too! You are left with just your skin and bones.

I laid in bed dreaming of food. I would find my boots and chew on the leather tongues. I dreamed that I was eating a big meal and felt happy for a short time. I even swallowed some parts of the leather.

Some nights it was better to sleep outside. The smell of dead people and the crowded conditions inside were awful.

Some people would just sleep anywhere and wrap their blanket around themselves. You had to hang on to your blanket otherwise it was taken by another prisoner. Men would just give up and sit outside and freeze to death.

8. The Experiment

One day we were told we were getting treated for our health. The whole barracks had to line up to be given an injection. The line was very long.

We went into a room where a nurse and guards were injecting the men. The nurse put a cotton wool pad over the injection spot to stop the bleeding.

I saw a cotton pad on the floor and picked it up. I hid it and when my turn came, I moved in front of the guard with the cotton pad on my arm. He waved me outside.

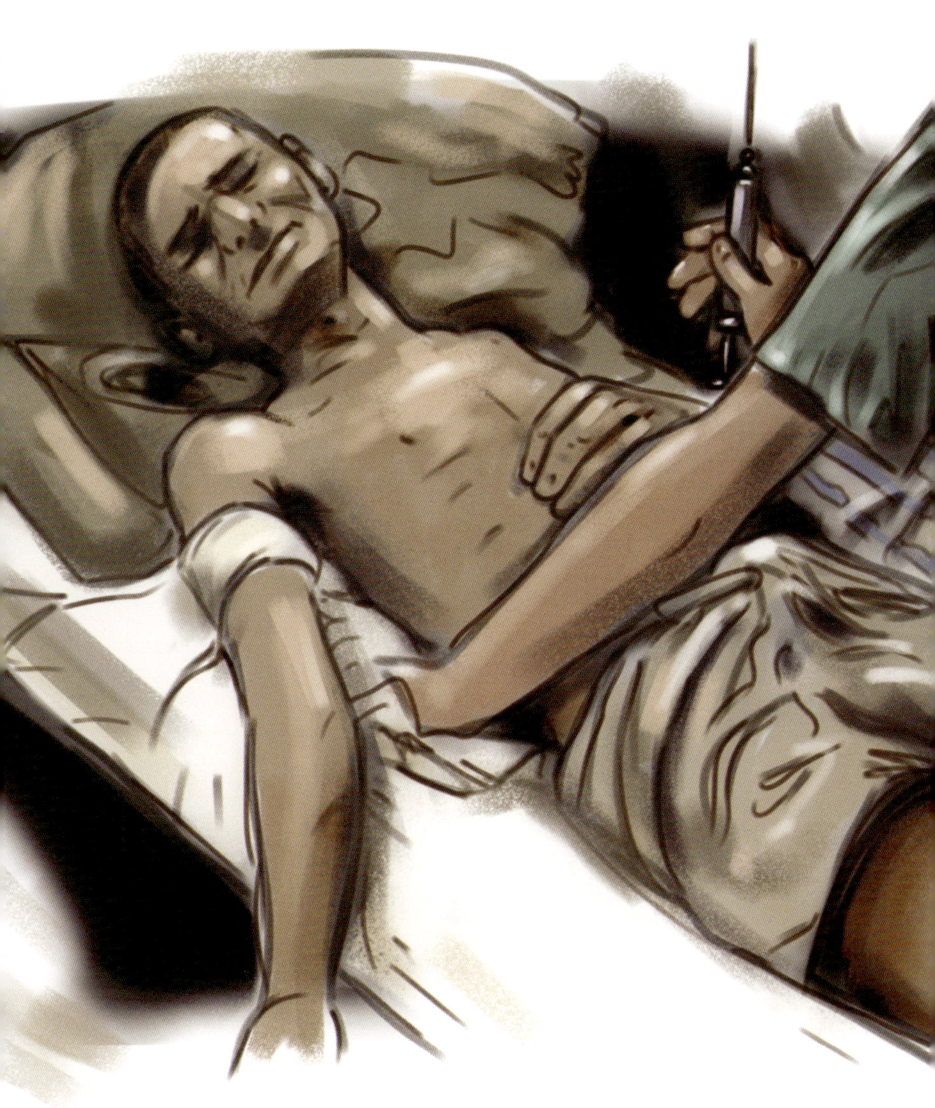

We were all taken back to the barracks to sleep. I went to bed as usual. I fell asleep and woke up in the middle of the night to silence.

I went back to sleep and woke up in the morning. All around me the men were still. Everyone was dead. I walked around looking at all the bodies.

Suddenly, the door burst open, and the guards came inside. They looked at me and got the doctors. The doctors could not believe I was still alive. They put me in the other barracks. I wanted to live!

33

The barracks was now filled with dead people left in their beds. Some people would go outside and sit around and die. Others would just die in their beds.

I tried to live and stole any food I could from the storeroom and kitchen. Scraps of bread and vegetables helped to keep me alive.

Some nights we could hear bombers flying overhead and explosions a long way off. We knew that the war had come to Germany. We had no idea how long it might take before we were free.

9. The Cold

The winter was freezing. I only had a blanket to wrap around me. I could never get warm.

I had to move around and find somewhere safe to keep me alive. I found some dead bodies in the barracks. I put the bodies together to put something between me and the ground. I slept on top of the dead people.

The smell of death was around you all day. The chimney put out black, oily smoke. You could smell and taste the smoke. It is a smell that you cannot forget. It was the smell of dead bodies burning.

The black smoke never stopped now. The people were dying all over the camp. I knew that I had to stay alive. I was too young to die.

10. Freedom

There was talk in the camp that the Americans were coming. We could hear guns and bombs exploding. One day we heard a big machine like a tank. But still no one came.

We were waiting and thought they would be here very soon. The guards were running away. We knew the Americans were coming but had to wait nearly a week for the soldiers to arrive.

The soldiers arrived and came through the gates. Some soldiers were vomiting and had tears in their eyes. Others were trying to help the dying prisoners.

I walked around to talk to the soldiers. One soldier was giving milk powder and chocolate to everyone. I did not eat it as it was poison to a starving body.

Another soldier gave me a handgun. He told me to go and shoot some Germans. I said to him that the war is over now and all I want to do is go home. I have forgiven, but I can never forget.

Word Bank

barracks	forgiven
Buchenwald	capture
concentration	experiment
Germany	Jewish
former	political
soldiers	disinfected
starving	separated
tongues	factories
bombers	survive
overhead	conditions
prisoners	injection
chocolate	Americans
explosion	